The 12 Step
Prayer Book

The 12 Step Prayer Book

A Collection of Favorite 12 Step Prayers
and Inspirational Readings

SECOND EDITION

Written and Compiled by

Bill P. and Lisa D.

HAZELDEN

Hazelden
Center City, Minnesota 55012-0176

1-800-328-0094
1-651-213-4590 (Fax)
www.hazelden.org

Library of Congress Cataloging-in-Publication Data

The twelve step prayer book : a collection of favorite
   twelve step prayers and inspirational readings /
   [edited by] Bill P. and Lisa D.—2nd ed.
      p. cm.
   ISBN -13: 987-1-59285-095-2

   1. Prayers. I. P., Bill, 1947– II. D., Lisa.

BV245T94 2004
204'.33—dc22
                                                    2004047284

08 07   6 5 4

Editor's Note
The Twelve Step Prayer Book is a companion volume to *Easy Does
It: A Book of Daily Twelve Step Meditations* written by Bill P.

Cover design by David Spohn
Interior design by Rachel Holscher

This book is dedicated
to the memory of

Patrick and Aimee Mott Butler

St. Paul, Minnesota

Contents

Step and Meeting Prayers

Inspirational Readings

New Prayers and Readings

Introduction

This collection of prayers and inspirational readings was written and compiled to assist members of all Twelve Step Fellowships with their prayer life and spiritual progress.

Those who are just beginning a life of recovery will find help with working the Eleventh Step. Those who have time in the Program will find a deepening of their spiritual life. Anyone who has trouble finding the "right words" to speak with their Higher Power may find exactly what they want to say in one of these prayers.

The table of contents will help in selecting a specific topic, and the Guide for Daily Reading offers an easy-to-follow method of using this book. We have added forty-four new prayers and readings in this second edition of *The Twelve Step Prayer Book*. You can find them in the "New Prayers and Readings" section, which begins with prayer #140 on page 107.

However you may define your Higher Power, may this collection be of assistance to you in your spiritual growth and recovery.

Guide for Daily Reading

Guide for Daily Reading

Guide for Daily Reading

Guide for Daily Reading

The 12 Step
Prayer Book

1
Serenity Prayer

God, grant me
The serenity to accept the things I cannot change;
The courage to change the things I can;
The wisdom to know the difference.
Living one day at a time;
Enjoying one moment at a time;
Accepting hardship as the pathway to peace;
Taking, as He did, this sinful world as it is, not as I
    would have it;
Trusting that He will make all things right if I sur-
    render to His will;
That I may be reasonably happy in this life, and
    supremely happy with Him forever in the next.

2
The Lord's Prayer

Our Father, Who art in heaven, hallowed be Thy
Name. Thy kingdom come. Thy will be done, on
earth as it is in heaven. Give us this day our daily
bread. And forgive us our trespasses, as we forgive
those who trespass against us. And lead us not into

temptation, but deliver us from evil. For Thine is the kingdom and the power and the glory, forever and ever. Amen.

3
Prayer of Saint Francis of Assisi

Lord, make me an instrument of Your peace!
Where there is hatred, let me sow love.
Where there is injury, pardon.
Where there is doubt, faith.
Where there is despair, hope.
Where there is darkness, light.
Where there is sadness, joy.
O Divine Master, grant that I may not so much seek
To be consoled as to console.
To be understood as to understand.
To be loved as to love.
For it is in giving that we receive.
It is in pardoning that we are pardoned.
It is in dying that we are born to eternal life.

4
Today's Thought

I am but one, but I am one;
I can't do everything,
But I can do SOMETHING;
What I can do, I ought to do,
What I ought to do, God helping me,
I WILL DO.

5
Sanskrit Proverb

Look to this day,
For it is life,
The very life of life.
In its brief course lies all
The realities and verities of existence,
The bliss of growth,
The splendor of action,
The glory of power.
For yesterday is but a dream,
And tomorrow is only a vision.
But today, well lived,
Makes every yesterday a dream of happiness

And every tomorrow a vision of hope.
Look well, therefore, to this day.

6
To Be Prayer

O Lord, I ain't what I ought to be,
And I ain't what I want to be,
And I ain't what I'm going to be,
But O Lord, I thank You
That I ain't what I used to be.

7
Prayer for the Hurried

Lord, slow me down.

Ease the pounding of my heart by quieting my mind. Steady my hurried pace. Give me, in the confusion of my day, the calmness of the everlasting hills. Break the tension of my nerves and muscles. Help me to know the magical, restoring power of sleep.

Teach me to take minute vacations by slowing down to look at a flower or a cloud, to chat with a friend, to pat a dog, to read a few lines from a good book. Remind me that the race is not always to the swift; that there is more to life than increasing speed.

Let me look upward into the branches of the towering oak and know that it grew great and strong because it grew slowly and well.

Lord, slow me down. Inspire me to send my roots deep into the soil of life's enduring values that I may grow toward the stars of my great destiny.

————————————

8
For Another Day

Thank You, dear God, for another day,
The chance to live in a decent way,
To feel again the joy of living,
And happiness that comes from giving.
Thank You for friends who can understand
And the peace that flows from Your loving hand.
Help me to wake to the morning sun
With the prayer, "Today Thy will be done,"
For with Your help I will find the way.
Thank You again, dear God, for another day.

9
The 23rd-1/2 Psalm

The Lord is my sponsor! I shall not want.

He directs me to go to many meetings.

He desires me to sit back, relax, and listen with an open mind.

He restores my soul, my sanity, and my health.

He leads me in the paths of sobriety, serenity, and fellowship for my own sake.

He teaches me to think, to take it easy, to live and let live, and to do first things first.

He makes me honest, humble, and grateful.

He teaches me to accept the things I cannot change, to change the things that I can, and gives me the wisdom to know the difference.

Yea, though I walk through the valley of despair, frustration, guilt, and remorse, I will fear no evil, for God is with me. The Program, God's way of life, the Twelve Steps—they comfort me.

God prepares a table before me in the presence of my enemies: rationalization, fear, anxiety, self-pity, and resentment.

God anoints my confused mind and jangled nerves with knowledge, understanding, and hope. No

longer am I alone; neither am I afraid, nor sick,
   nor helpless, nor hopeless. My cup runneth over.
Surely sobriety and serenity shall follow me every
   day of my life, twenty-four hours at a time, as I
   surrender my will to God and carry the message
   to others; and I will dwell in the house of my
   Higher Power, as I understand Him, daily.
   Forever and Ever. Amen.

10
This I Believe

Tomorrow is yet to be,
But should God grant me another day,
The Hope, Courage, and Strength
Through the working of the Twelve Steps and
   Serenity Prayer,
I shall be sufficiently provided for to meet my
   every need.
This I believe.

11
No Greater Power

To find direction and meaning I must tap a Higher Power. That Power is God as I understand Him. I will start each day with God and take Steps Three, Seven, and Eleven. There is no Greater Power. And then I say:

Lord, I turn my life and will over to You today.

I will walk humbly with You and my fellow travelers.

You are giving me a grateful heart for my many blessings.

You are directing my thinking and separating me from self-pity, dishonesty, and self-seeking motives.

You are removing my resentments, fears, and other character defects that stand in my way.

You are giving me freedom from self-will.

Your will, Lord, not mine.

You will show me today what I can do to help someone who is still hurting.

As I go out today to do Your bidding,

You are helping me to become a better person.

12
The Beatitudes

Blessed are the poor in spirit, for theirs is the
kingdom of heaven.

Blessed are they who mourn, for they shall be
comforted.

Blessed are the meek, for they shall inherit the earth.

Blessed are they who hunger and thirst after righ-
teousness, for they shall be filled.

Blessed are the merciful, for they shall obtain mercy.

Blessed are the pure in heart, for they shall see God.

Blessed are the peacemakers, for they shall be called
the children of God.

Blessed are they who are persecuted for righteous-
ness's sake, for theirs is the kingdom of heaven.

13
The Tolerance Prayer

Lord, give me tolerance toward those whose thoughts
and ways, in the Program and life, conflict with mine.
For though I would, I cannot always know what con-
stitutes the Absolute Truth. The other person may be
right, while I may be all wrong, yet unaware.

Lord, make my motives right, for only this can ease my conscience when I sometimes err.

Lord, give me tolerance, for who am I to stand in judgment on another person's mistakes? No one knows better than my inward self how many little blunders I have and can make.

Life is full of stones that somehow trip us, and meaning not, we stumble now and then.

Lord, give me tolerance, for only You are rightly fit to judge my fellow travelers.

14
A Beginner's Prayer

Lord, I want to love You, yet I am not sure.
I want to trust You, yet I am afraid of being taken in.
I know I need You, but I am ashamed of the need.
I want to pray, but I am afraid of being a hypocrite.
I need my independence, yet I fear to be alone.
I want to belong, yet I must be myself.
Take me, Lord, yet leave me alone.
Lord, I believe; help me with my unbelief.
O Lord, if You are there, You do understand,
    don't You?
Give me what I need, but leave me free to choose.

Help me work it out my own way, but don't let me go.
Let me understand myself, but don't let me despair.
Come unto me, O Lord, I want You there.
Lighten my darkness, but don't dazzle me.
Help me to see what I need to do, and give me
    strength to do it.
O Lord, I believe; help me with my unbelief.

15
God, Help Me Live Today

God, more than anything else in this world, I just
    don't want to be sick any more.
God, grant me the serenity to accept the things I
    cannot change (people, places, and things),
The courage to change the things I can (my attitudes),
And the common sense to know the difference.
God, help me please to stay clean and sober this day,
    even if it's in spite of myself. Help me, Lord, to
    stay sensitive to my own needs and the things that
    are good for me, and to stay sensitive to the needs
    of others and the things that are good for them.
And if You please, Lord, free me enough of the
    bondage of self that I may be of some useful value
    as a human being, whether I understand or not,

That I may carry my own keys, maintain my own integrity, and live this day at peace with You, at peace with myself, and at peace with the world I live in, just for today.

God help me during this day to demonstrate that:

It is good for me to love and to be loved.

It is good for me to understand and to be understood.

It is good for me to give and to receive.

It is good for me to comfort and to allow myself to be comforted.

And it is obviously far better for me to be useful as a human being, than it is to be selfish.

God, help me please to put one foot in front of the other, to keep moving forward, and to do the best I can with what I have to work with today,

Accepting the results of whatever that may or may not be.

16
O God of Our Understanding

This is the dawn of a new day in the Program. I shall thank You, my Higher Power, for last night's rest, Your gift.

Yesterday is gone, except for what I have learned

from it, good or bad. Today I have the same choice, a Divine privilege which swells my heart with hope and purpose. This is my day, the purity of a new beginning.

I will receive from this day exactly what I give to it. As I do good things, good will be done to me. It is my gift to mold into something everlasting and to do those things which will affect the people around me in an ever-widening circle. The worthiness of this effort rests entirely with me.

This is my day for love, because I know that as I love, I will be loved. Hate and jealousy cannot exist in the presence of love. I will be sustained by this miracle of Your creation and this day will be lightened by my love for others and especially love for my fellow travelers in the Program.

Today I will do my best without thought of failures of the past or anxieties for the future. When this day is ended, I will have no regrets. On retiring I shall thank You, my Higher Power, for this wonderful day.

17
The Acceptance Prayer

God grant me the serenity to accept my addiction gracefully and humbly. Grant me also the ability to absorb the teachings of the Program, which by its past experience is trying to help me. Teach me to be grateful for the help I receive.

Guide me, Higher Power, in the path of tolerance and understanding of my fellow members and fellow-man, guide me away from the path of criticism, intolerance, jealousy, and envy of my friends. Let me not prejudge; let me not become a moralist; keep my tongue and thoughts from malicious, idle gossip.

Help me to grow in stature spiritually, mentally, and morally. Grant me that greatest of all rewards, that of being able to help my fellow sufferers in their search out of the addiction that has encompassed them.

Above all, help me to be less critical and impatient with myself.

18
The Twelve Steps Prayer

Power, greater than myself, as I understand You, I willingly admit that without Your help I am powerless over alcohol and my life has become unmanageable. I believe You can restore me to sanity. I turn my life and my will over to You. I have made a searching and fearless moral inventory of myself and I admit to You, to myself, and to another the exact nature of my wrongs. I am entirely ready to have You remove these defects of character. I humbly ask You to remove my shortcomings. I have made direct amends to all persons I have harmed, except when to do so would injure them or others. I will continue to take personal inventory and when I am wrong I will promptly admit it. I seek through prayer and meditation to improve my conscious contact with You and pray only for knowledge of Your will for me and the power to carry it out.

Grant me the grace to carry the message of Your help unto others and to practice the principles of the Twelve Steps in all my affairs.

19
The Victims of Addiction

O blessed Lord, You ministered to all who came to You.

Look with compassion upon all who through addiction have lost their health and freedom. Restore to them the assurance of Your unfailing mercy; remove from them the fears that beset them; strengthen them in the work of their recovery; and to those who care for them, give patient understanding and persevering love.

20
God's Answer

I asked You, God, for strength that I might achieve;
I was made weak that I might learn humbly to obey.
I asked for help that I might do greater things;
I was given infirmity that I might do better things.
I asked for riches that I might be happy;
I was given poverty that I might be wise.
I asked for power that I might have the praise of
     men;
I was given weakness that I might feel the need for
     You.
I asked for all things that I might enjoy life;
I was given life that I might enjoy all things.
No, dear Lord, I've gotten nothing that I asked for;
But everything I had hoped for.
Despite myself, my prayers were answered;
And I am among those most richly blessed.

21
Every Morning

Every morning I will rest my arms awhile upon the windowsill of heaven, gaze upon my Higher Power, and with that vision in my heart turn strong to meet my day.

22
Sobriety Prayer

If I speak in the tongues of men and even of angels, but have not sobriety, I am a noisy gong or a clanging cymbal. And if I have prophetic powers, and understand all mysteries and all knowledge, and if I have all faith, so as to move mountains but have not sobriety, I am nothing. If I give away all that I have, and if I deliver my body to be burned, but have not sobriety, I gain nothing.

When I am sober, I am patient and kind. When I am sober, I am not jealous nor boastful, nor arrogant or rude. When I am sober, I do not insist on my own way. When I am sober, I am not irritable or resentful. I do not rejoice at wrong as I used to do but rejoice in what is right.

When I am sober, I can bear all things, believe in all things, hope all things, and endure all things.

Sobriety never ends and never fails.

When I was using, I spoke like an arrogant child, thought like a stubborn child, and reasoned like a rebellious child. When I chose sobriety for my life, I gave up my childish ways.

So faith, hope, love, and sobriety abide, but for me, the most important has to be sobriety, for without it, I cannot have the other three, nor can I ever have the serenity I yearn to possess.

23
Fellow Travelers

Higher Power, Who fills our whole life, and Whose presence we find wherever we go, preserve us who travel the road of recovery, surround us with Your loving care, protect us from every danger, and bring us safely to our journey's end.

24
My First Prayer

I surrender to Thee my entire life, O God of my understanding. I have made a mess of it, trying to run it myself. You take it, the whole thing, and run it for me, according to Your will and plan.

25
Possibilities Prayer

I know, dear God, that my part in this Program is going to be a thrilling and endless adventure. Despite all that has happened to me already, I know that I have just begun to grow. I have just begun to open to Your love. I have just begun to touch the varied lives You are using me to change. I have just begun to sense the possibilities ahead. And these possibilities, I am convinced, will continue to unfold into ever new and richer adventures, not only for the rest of my reborn days but also through eternity.

26
Enough to Need

Dear God, never allow me to think that I have
knowledge enough to need no teaching, wisdom
enough to need no correction, talents enough
to need no grace, goodness enough to need no
progress, humility enough to need no repentance,
devotion enough to need no improvement, strength
sufficient without Thy Spirit, lest, standing still, I
fall back forevermore.

27
The Gifts I Ask

These are the gifts I ask of Thee,
Spirit Serene:
Strength for the daily task,
Courage to face the road,
Good cheer to help me
Bear the traveler's load;
And for the hours that come between,
An inward joy in all things heard and seen.

28
Peace in God's Will

My Higher Power, quicken my spirit and fix my thoughts on Your will, that I may see what You would have done, and contemplate its doing without self-consciousness or inner excitement, without haste and without delay, without fear of other people's judgments or anxiety about success, knowing only that it is Your will and therefore must be done quietly, faithfully, and lovingly, for in Your will alone is my peace.

29
For Those Who Have Relapsed

O God of all mercies and comfort, Who helps us in time of need, we humbly ask You to behold, visit, and relieve those who have relapsed for whom our prayers are desired. Look upon them with the eyes of Your mercy; comfort them with a sense of Your goodness; preserve them from the temptations of their addiction; and give them patience under their affliction. In Your time, restore them to the Program and physical, mental, and spiritual health. And help them, we pray, to listen, believe, and do Your will.

30
Thank You, God

Thank You, God, for all You have given me.
Thank You for all You have taken from me.
But, most of all, I thank You, God, for what You've left me:
Recovery, along with peace of mind, faith, hope, and love.

31
Humility Prayer

Lord, I am far too much influenced by what people think of me;
   Which means that I am always pretending to be either richer or smarter than I really am. Please prevent me from trying to attract attention.
   Don't let me gloat over praise on the one hand

and be discouraged by criticism on the other, nor let me waste time weaving the most imaginary situations in which the heroic, charming, witty person present is myself.

Show me how to be humble of heart.

32
My Daily Prayer

God, I turn my will and my life over to You this day for Your keeping. Your will, Lord, not mine. I ask for Your guidance and direction. I will walk humbly with You and Your fellowman. You are giving me a grateful heart for my many blessings. You are removing the defects of character that stand in my way. You are giving me freedom from self-will.

Let love, compassion, and understanding be in my every thought, word, and deed this day. I release those to You who have mistreated me. I truly desire Your abundance of truth, love, harmony, and peace. As I go out today to do Your bidding, let me help anyone I can who is less fortunate than I.

33
Lord, I'm Hurting

Yes, Lord, I hurt.
The pain is deep,
And I feel the mountains
Are so steep.
I cannot seem to stand.
Please, dear Lord,
Take my hand.
I cannot seem to find my way.
For me the sun
Is not shining today.
I know You're there;
I've felt Your presence near
But now, my Lord,
My heart is gripped with fear.
Lord, help the sun to shine
And to know
That You are mine.
Heal this pain I feel;
Make Your presence
Very real.
Today, Lord, I give You all.
Help me, dear Lord,
Not to fall.
And if I fall,
Hold me tight,

So I can feel
Your strength and might.

34
The Right Road

Dear God,
I have no idea where I am going.
I do not see the road ahead of me.
I cannot know for certain where it will end.
Nor do I really know myself, and the fact that I am
    actually doing so.
But I believe this.
I believe that the desire to please You does in fact
    please You.
I hope I have that desire in everything I do.
I hope I never do anything apart from that desire.
And I know that if I do this, You will lead me by the
    right road though I may know nothing about it at
    the time.
Therefore, I will trust You always, for though I may
    seem to be lost, and in the shadow of death, I will
    not be afraid, because I know You will never
    leave me to face my troubles alone.

35
O Great Spirit

O Great Spirit,

Whose voice I hear in the winds, and whose breath gives life to all the world, hear me! I am small and weak, I need Your strength and wisdom. Let me walk in beauty, and make my eyes ever behold the red and purple sunset.

Make my hands respect the things You have made, and my ears sharp to hear Your voice.

Make me wise so that I may understand the things You have taught my people.

Let me learn the lessons You have hidden in every leaf and rock.

I seek strength, not to be greater than my brother, but to fight my greatest enemy: myself.

Make me always ready to come to You with clean hands and straight eyes.

So when life fades, as the fading sunset, my spirit may come to You without shame.

36
A Prayer for Tolerance

Higher Power, help me to know the most lovable quality I can possess is tolerance. It is the vision that enables me to see things from another's viewpoint. It is the generosity that concedes to others the right to their own opinions and their own peculiarities. It is the bigness that enables me to let people be happy in their own way instead of my way.

37
Changes

Today I pray that I may understand there are some
    things I cannot change:
I cannot change the weather.
I cannot change the tick of the clock.
I cannot change the past.
I cannot change another person against his or her
    will.
I cannot change what is right and wrong.
I cannot change the fact that a relationship ended.
I can stop worrying over that which I cannot change
    and enjoy living more! I can place those things

into the hands of my Higher Power. Save energy.
Let go. Instead of trying to change someone else:
I can change my attitude.
I can change my list of priorities.
I can change my bad habits into good ones.
I can move from the place of brokenness into wholeness, in the beautiful person God created me to become.

38
Take Time

Today I pray that I can:
Take time to think.
> It is the source of power.
Take time to play.
> It is the secret of perpetual youth.
Take time to read.
> It is the fountain of wisdom.
Take time to pray.
> It is the greatest power on earth.
Take time to be friendly.
> It is the road to happiness.
Take time to laugh.
> It is the music of the soul.

Take time to give.
    It is too short a day to be selfish.
Take time to work.
    It is the price of success.
Take time to do charity.
    It is the key to heaven.

39
Life Is a Celebration

Lord, help me today to:
Mend a quarrel.
Seek out a forgotten friend.
Dismiss suspicion and replace it with trust.
Write a friendly letter.
Share a treasure.
Give a soft answer.
Encourage another.
Manifest my loyalty in word and deed.
Keep a promise.
Find the time.
Forego a grudge.
Forgive an enemy.
Listen.
Acknowledge any wrongdoing.

Try to understand.
Examine my demands on others.
Think of someone else first.
Be kind.
Be gentle.
Laugh a little.
Smile more.
Be happy.
Show my gratitude.
Welcome a stranger.
Speak Your love.
Speak it again.
Live it again.
LIFE IS A CELEBRATION!

40
Language of the Heart

Dear God, You know my needs before I ask, my heart before I pray, and my gratitude before I even offer my thanks. You understand me better than I understand myself, and I thank You for communicating with me in the language of the heart.

41
Am I Willing?

Dear Higher Power, help me:

To forget what I have done for other people, and to remember what other people have done for me.

To ignore what the world owes me, and to think what I owe the world.

To put my rights in the background, and my duties in the middle distance, and my chances to do a little more than my duty in the foreground.

To see that my fellow members are just as real as I am, and to try to look behind their faces to their hearts, as hungry for joy as mine is.

To own that probably the only good reason for my existence is not what I can get out of life, but what I can give to life.

To close my book of complaints against the management of the universe and look for a place where I can sow a few seeds of happiness—am I willing to do these things even for a day?

Then I have a good chance of staying with the Program.

42
The Way

Dear Lord, today I pray:
The way is long
Let us go together.
The way is difficult
Let us help each other.
The way is joyful
Let us share it.
The way is ours alone
Let us go in love.
The way grows before us
Let us begin.

43
On Awakening

God, please direct my thinking, especially move it from self-pity, dishonest and self-seeking motives.

As I go through the day and face indecision, please give me the inspiration, an intuitive thought, or a decision. Make me relax and take it easy; don't let me struggle. Let me rely upon Your inspiration, intuitive thoughts, and decision instead of my old ideas.

Show me all through the day what my next step is to be and give me whatever I need to take care of each problem. God, I ask You especially for freedom from self-will and I make no requests for myself only. But give me the knowledge of Your will for me and the power to carry it out in every contact during the day.

As I go through this day, let me pause when agitated or doubtful and ask You for the right thought or action. Let me constantly be reminded that I am no longer running the show, humbly saying many times each day, "Thy will be done" and agreeing that it is.

I will then be in much less danger of excitement, fear, anger, worry, self-pity, or foolish decisions. I will be more efficient. I won't be burning up energy foolishly as I was when trying to run life to suit myself. I will let You discipline me in this simple way. I will give You all the responsibility and all the praise.

44
A Morning Prayer

Good morning, God. You are ushering in another
    day, all nice and freshly new.
Here I come again, dear Lord. Please renew me too.
Forgive the many errors that I made yesterday

And let me come again, dear God, to walk in Your
   own way.
But, God, You know I cannot do it on my own.
Please take my hand and hold it tight, for I cannot
   walk alone.

45
Who, Me?

I need to be forgiven, Lord, so many times a day.
So often do I stumble and fall. Be merciful, I pray.
Help me to not be critical when others' faults I see.
For so often, Lord, the same faults are in me.

46
Let Go, Let God

Higher Power, help me to understand:
To "let go" does not mean to stop caring, it means I
   can't do it for someone else.
To "let go" is not to enable, but to allow learning
   from natural consequences.

To "let go" is to admit powerlessness, which means
the outcome is not in my hands.

To "let go" is not to try to change or blame another,
it's to make the most of myself.

To "let go" is not to care for but to care about.

To "let go" is not to fix but to be supportive.

To "let go" is not to judge but to allow another to be
a human being.

To "let go" is not to protect, it's to permit another to
face reality.

To "let go" is not to deny but to accept.

To "let go" is not to nag, scold, or argue but instead
to search out my own shortcomings and correct
them.

To "let go" is not to adjust everything to my desires
but to take each day as it comes and cherish myself in it.

47
As I Think

Higher Power, today with Your help I'll remember:

As I think, I travel; and as I love, I attract. I am
today where my thoughts have brought me; I will
be tomorrow where my thoughts take me. I cannot

escape the result of my thoughts, but I can endure and learn; I can accept and be glad. I will realize the vision (not the idle wish) of my heart, be it base or beautiful, or a mixture of both; for I will always gravitate toward that which I, secretly, most love. Into my hands will be placed the exact result of my thoughts; I will receive that which I earn, no more, no less. Whatever my present environment may be, I will fall, remain, or rise with my thoughts, my vision, my attitudes. I will become as small as my controlling desire, as great as my dominant aspiration.

48
I Cannot Pray

I cannot pray the Lord's Prayer and even once say "I."
I cannot pray the Lord's Prayer and even once
    say "my."
Nor can I pray the Lord's Prayer and not pray for
    another,
And when I ask for daily bread, I must include my
    brother.
For others are included in each and every plea,
From the beginning to the end of it, it does not once
    say "me."

49
Lead Me and Guide Me

Almighty God, I humbly pray,
Lead me and guide me through this day.
Cast out my selfishness and sin,
Open my heart to let You in.
Help me now as I blindly stray
Over the pitfalls along the way.
Let me have courage to face each task,
Invest me with patience and love, I ask.
Care for me through each hour today,
Strengthen and guard me now, I pray.

As I forgive, forgive me too,
Needing Your mercy as I do.
Oh, give me Your loving care,
Never abandon me to despair.
Yesterday's wrongs I would seek to right,
Make me more perfect in Your sight.
Oh, teach me to live as best I can,
Use me to help my fellowman.
Save me from acts of bitter shame,
    I humbly ask it in Your name.

50
The Universal Prayer

Eternal Reality,
You are everywhere.
You are infinite unity, truth, and love;
You permeate our souls,
Every corner of the universe, and beyond.

To some of us, You are father, friend, or partner.
To others, Higher Power, Higher Self, or Inner Self.
To many of us, You are all these and more.
You are within us and we within You.

We know You forgive our trespasses
If we forgive ourselves and others.
We know You protect us from destructive temptation
If we continue to seek Your help and guidance.
We know You provide us food and shelter today
If we but place our trust in You and try to do our best.
Give us this day knowledge of Your will for us and
     the power to carry it out.
For Yours, is infinite power and love,
Forever.

51
Reliance on God

O Higher Power,
Never let me think
that I can stand by myself,
and not need You.

52
Sailor's Prayer

Dear God, be good to me. The sea is so wide, and
my boat is so small.

53
An Irish Blessing

May the road rise to meet you,
May the wind be always at your back,
May the sun shine warm upon your face,

The rain fall softly on your fields,
And until we meet again,
May God hold you in the palm of His hand.

———————————

54
First Things First

Dear Higher Power, remind me:
To tidy up my own mind,
To keep my sense of values straight,
To sort out the possible and the impossible,
To turn the impossible over to You,
And get busy on the possible.

———————————

55
Open Mind

Higher Power, may I understand:
To be alert to my own needs, not to the faults of
    others;
To remain teachable;
To listen;

To keep an open mind; and
To learn not who's right but what's right.

———————————————

56
Do the Right Thing

Help me, Higher Power, to get out of myself, to
stop always thinking what I need. Show me the way
I can be helpful to others and supply me with the
strength to do the right thing.

———————————————

57
Run the Race

Help me this day, Higher Power, to run with
patience the race that is set before me.

May neither opposition without nor discourage-
ment within divert me from my progress in recovery.

Inspire in me strength of mind, willingness, and
acceptance, that I may meet all fears and difficulties
with courage, and may complete the tasks set before
me today.

58
True Power

Take from me, Higher Power, my false pride and
grandiosity, all my phoniness and self-importance,
and help me find the courage that shows itself in
gentleness, the wisdom that shows itself in simplic-
ity, and the true power that shows itself in modesty
and humility.

59
Prayer for Protection

The light of God surrounds me;
The love of God enfolds me;
The power of God protects me;
The presence of God watches over me;
Wherever I am, God is!

60
The Gratitude Prayer

O God,
I want to thank You for bringing me this far along
  the road to recovery.
It is good to be able to get my feet on the floor again.
It is good to be able to do at least some things for
  myself again.
Best of all is to have the joy of feeling well again.
O God,
Keep me grateful;
Grateful to all of the people who helped me back to
  health;
Grateful to You for the way in which You have
  brought me through it all.
O God,
Give me patience.
Help me to not be in too big a hurry to do too much.
Help me to keep on doing what I'm told to do.
Help me to be so obedient to those who know what
  is best for me, that very soon I shall be on the top
  of the world and on the top of my job again.
I can say what the psalmist said:
"I waited patiently for the Lord;
He inclined to me and heard my cry.
He took me from a fearful pit, and from the miry clay,
And on a rock He set my feet, establishing my way."

61
No Other

I have no other helper than You,
  no other father,
  no other redeemer,
  no other support.
I pray to You.
Only You can help me.
My present misery is too great.
Despair grips me, and I am at my wits' end.
I am sunk in the depths, and I cannot pull myself up
  or out.
If it is Your will, help me out of this misery.
Let me know that You are stronger than all misery
  and all enemies.
O Lord, if I come through this, please let the experi-
  ence contribute to my and my brothers' blessings.
You will not forsake me; this I know.

62
All That We Ought

All that we ought to have thought and have not
  thought,

All that we ought to have said and have not said,
All that we ought to have done and have not done;
All that we ought not to have thought and yet have
thought,
All that we ought not to have spoken and yet have
spoken,
All that we ought not to have done and yet have done;
For thoughts, words, and works, pray we, O God,
for forgiveness,
And repent with penance.

63
Love

Higher Power, remind me that:
Love is patient;
Love is kind.
Love is not jealous; it does not put on airs; it is not
snobbish.
Love is never rude; it is not self-seeking; it is not
prone to anger; neither does it brood over injuries.
Love does not rejoice in what is wrong, but rejoices
with the truth.
There is no limit to love's forbearance, its truth, its
hope, its power to endure.

64
Help Me Remember

Lord,
Help me remember that nothing is going to happen
    to me today that You and I together can't handle.

65
The Twelve Rewards

Spirit of the Universe,
I humbly ask for Your help so I may continue to
    realize the rewards of recovery:
1. Hope instead of desperation.
2. Faith instead of despair.
3. Courage instead of fear.
4. Peace of mind instead of confusion.
5. Self-respect instead of self-contempt.
6. Self-confidence instead of helplessness.
7. The respect of others instead of pity and
    contempt.
8. A clean conscience instead of a sense of guilt.
9. Real friendship instead of loneliness.

10. A clean pattern of life instead of a purposeless existence.
11. The love and understanding of my family instead of their doubts and fears.
12. The freedom of a happy life instead of the bondage of addiction.

66
New Day

Thank You, God, for today.

This is the beginning of a new day. I can waste it or use it for good.

What I do today is important because I am exchanging a day of my life for it.

When tomorrow comes, this day will be gone forever—leaving in its place something I have traded for it.

I want it to be gain, not loss; good, not evil; success, not failure; in order that I shall not regret the price I paid for today.

67
Release Me

Lord, keep me from the habit of thinking I must say something on every subject and on every occasion.

Release me from wanting to control everyone's affairs.

Keep my mind free from the recital of endless details—give me wings to get to the point.

I ask for grace enough to listen to the tales of others' pains. Help me to endure them with patience, but seal my lips on my own aches and pains—they are increasing and my love of rehearsing them is becoming sweeter as the years go by.

Teach me the glorious lesson that occasionally it is possible that I may be mistaken.

Keep me reasonably sweet. I do not want to be a saint—some of them are so difficult to live with—but a sour old person is one of the crowning works of the devil.

Give me the ability to see good things in unexpected places, and talents in unexpected people. And give me, O Lord, the grace to tell them so.

Make me thoughtful, but not moody; helpful, but not bossy. With my vast store of wisdom, it seems a pity to not use it all, but you know, Lord, that I want a few friends at the end.

68
Please, Lord

Please, Lord, teach us to laugh again; but God, don't
ever let us forget that we cried.

69
My Prayer for You

I thought of you so much today
I went to God in prayer,
To ask Him to watch over you
And show you that we care.

My prayer for you was not for rewards
That you could touch or feel,
But true rewards for happiness
That are so very real.

Like love and understanding
In all the things you do,
And guidance when you need it most
To see your troubles through.

I asked Him for good health for you
So your future could be bright,
And faith to accept life's challenges
And the courage to do what's right.

I gave thanks to Him
For granting my prayer
To bring you peace and love.
May you feel the warmth in your life
With God's blessings from above.

———————————————

70
Self-Respect Prayer

O God, teach me that self-respect cannot be hunted.
It cannot be purchased. It is never for sale. It comes
to me when I am alone, in quiet moments, in quiet
places, when I suddenly realize that, knowing the
good, I have done it; knowing the beautiful, I have
served it; knowing the truth, I have spoken it.

71
Do It Now

Dear God,

I expect to pass through this world but once.

Any good thing, therefore, that I can do, or any kindness I can show to any fellow traveler, let me do it now.

Let me not defer nor neglect it, for I shall not pass this way again.

72
To Change

I pray that I may continue to change, and I appreciate You for investing in me Your time, Your patience, Your understanding; and for seeing in me someone worthwhile. I am sorry for the past—but I will change for the better, and I am grateful for the opportunity.

73
Unselfishness Prayer

Higher Power, guide me as I walk the narrow way between being selfish and unselfish. I know I must be selfish, to concentrate on my own recovery, so I do not slip and be of no use to myself or anyone else. Yet I must also be unselfish, reaching out to others, sensitive to their needs, and willing to meet them at any time. With Your help, I can do both, and keep a balance that will give me a proper perspective in my life.

74
Light a Candle

O God of my understanding, light a candle within my heart, that I may see what is therein and remove the wreckage of the past.

75
What Is Best

O Lord, You know what is best for me. Let this or
that be done, as you please. Give what You will,
how much You will, and when You will.

76
Prayer for Healing

Higher Power,

You have told us to ask and we will receive, to
seek and we will find, to knock and You will open
the door to us.

I trust in Your love for me and in the healing
power of Your compassion. I praise You and thank
You for the mercy You have shown to me.

Higher Power, I am sorry for all my mistakes. I ask
for Your help in removing the negative patterns of my
life. I accept with all my heart Your forgiving love.

I ask for the grace to be aware of the character
defects that exist within myself. Let me not offend
You by my weak human nature, or by my impatience,
resentment, or neglect of people who are a part of
my life. Rather, teach me the gift of understanding

and the ability to forgive, just as You continue to forgive me.

I seek Your strength and Your peace so that I may become Your instrument in sharing those gifts with others.

Guide me in my prayer that I might know what needs to be healed and how to ask You for that healing.

It is You, Higher Power, whom I seek. Please enter the door of my heart and fill me with the presence of Your spirit now and forever.

I thank You, God, for doing this.

77
Things to Give

Today, I pray I may give:

To my enemy:	Forgiveness.
To my opponent:	Tolerance.
To my customer:	Service.
To a friend:	Kindness.
To all people:	Charity.
To my family:	My heart.
To every child:	A good example.
To myself:	Respect.

To You, Higher Power: **LOVE**
With all my heart,
With all my soul,
With all my mind.

78
Your Gift

Thank You, Higher Power, for Your gift of recovery; that through this Program I have come to know myself better than ever before, and that I have come to know others better as well. I pray that I may be eternally grateful for this, Your blessing.

79
I Promise Myself!

Today I pray:

To promise myself to be so strong that nothing can disturb my peace of mind.

To talk health, happiness, and prosperity to every person I meet.

To make all of my friends feel that there is something in them.

To look at the sunny side of everything and make my optimism come true.

To think only of the best, to work only for the best, and to expect only the best.

To be just as enthusiastic about the success of others as I am about my own.

To forget the mistakes of the past and press on to the greater achievements of the future.

To wear a cheerful countenance at all times and give every living creature I meet a smile.

To give so much time to the improvement of myself that I have no time to criticize others.

To be too large for worry, too noble for anger, too strong for fear, and too happy to permit the presence of trouble.

80
My Worth

I pray to remember that my worth is not determined by my show of outward strength, or the volume of my voice, or the thunder of my accomplishments. It is to be seen, rather, in terms of the nature and depth of my commitments, the genuineness of my friendships, the sincerity of my purpose, the quiet courage of my convictions, my capacity to accept life on life's terms, and my willingness to continue "growing up." This I pray.

81
Right Living

Higher Power, deliver me:
From the cowardice that dare not face new truth;
From the laziness that is contented with half-truth;
From the arrogance that thinks it knows all truth;
These things, good Lord, that I pray for,
Give me the strength to work for.

82
Against Temptations

May the strength of my Higher Power guide me.
May the power of God preserve me.
May the wisdom of my Higher Power instruct me.

May the hand of God protect me.
May the way of my Higher Power direct me.
May His shield defend me.
And may the presence of, and belief in, my Higher
 Power guard me against the temptations of the
 world.

———————————————

83
Prayer to Know

Grant it to me, Higher Power:
To know that which is worth knowing,
To love that which is worth loving,
To praise that which pleases You most,
To work for that which helps others.
Grant it to me:
To distinguish with true judgment things that differ,
 and above all to search out, and to do what is
 most pleasing to You.

84
Recovery Prayer

Today and every day, I pray to be ever mindful that recovery is the most important thing in my life, without exception. I may believe my job, or my home life, or one of many other things, comes first. But if I don't stay with the Program, chances are I won't have a job, a family, sanity, or even life. If I am convinced that everything in life depends on my recovery, I have a much better chance of improving my life. If I put other things first, I am only hurting my chances.

85
Kindness and Service

O Lord, help me always to remember thankfully the work of those who helped me when I needed help. Reward them for their kindness and service, and grant that I may have the will, the time, and the opportunity to do the same for others.

86
Make Me

God, who touches earth with beauty,
Make me lovely too;
With Your Spirit re-create me,
Make my heart anew.

Like Your springs and running waters,
Make me crystal pure;
Like Your rocks of towering grandeur
Make me strong and sure.

Like Your dancing waves in sunlight,
Make me glad and free;
Like the straightness of the pine trees
Let me upright be.

Like the arching of the heavens,
Lift my thoughts above;
Turn my dreams to noble action,
Ministries of love.

God, who touches earth with beauty,
Make me lovely too;
Keep me ever, by Your Spirit,
Pure and strong and true.

87
Guide Me

Thank You, Higher Power, for this beautiful day, for
strength, for health.
Help me to live this day for You.
Place in my path some way to serve others.
Help me to know that no other walks in my shoes;
that there is something that only I can do today.
Guide my thoughts and deeds that I may feel Your
presence today and in all the tomorrows.

88
Anniversary Prayer

Dear God, I had another anniversary today, one
more year in recovery. It has been difficult at times,
but it has allowed many blessings. I am a human
being again. I feel new strength in my body, spirit,
and mind. The world has never looked so good.
I have the respect of my friends and family. I am
productive in my work. I do not miss the slippery
people and places. When I have been tempted, You,
my Higher Power, have sustained me. I have found a

home in the Fellowship and friends support me. Stay close by me, God. I thank You. This is the life I love.

89
To Be Honest

Higher Power, help me to be honest with myself. It is so easy to alibi, to make excuses for my shortcomings. It is so easy to blame others and circumstances as a child does. Help me to see myself honestly: a human being who needs You this day and every day. Help me to surrender my weak will to Your strength.

90
Teach Me

Teach me, God, so that I might know
The way to change and the way to grow.
Give me the words to ask You how
To handle the here and live in the now.
Tempt me not with the valleys of death,
Give me freedom from fear in every breath.

And though mistakes I make in my daily life,
Deliver me from aiding strife.
Understand me, God, as I am now
And show me the furrows I need to plow
To reach my goal as a ripening food,
So I might feed others all that is good.
Fill me with energy known as the Power,
Until I come to rest at the midnight hour.

91
The Fellowship Prayer

Dear Higher Power, I am grateful that:
I am part of the Fellowship, one among many, but I
     am one.
I need to work the Steps for the development of the
     buried life within me.
Our Program may be human in its organization, but
     it is Divine in its purpose. The purpose is to con-
     tinue my spiritual awakening.
Participating in the privileges of the movement, I
     shall share in the responsibilities, taking it upon
     myself to carry my fair share of the load, not
     grudgingly, but joyfully.
To the extent that I fail in my responsibilities, the

Program fails. To the extent that I succeed, the Program succeeds.

I shall not wait to be drafted for service to my fellow members. I shall volunteer.

I shall be loyal in my attendance, generous in my giving, kind in my criticism, creative in my suggestions, loving in my attitudes.

I shall give to the Program my interest, my enthusiasm, my devotion, and, most of all, myself.

92
First Step Prayer

Today, I ask for help with my addiction. Denial has kept me from seeing how powerless I am and how my life is unmanageable. I need to learn and remember that I have an incurable illness and that abstinence is the only way to deal with it.

93
Second Step Prayer

I pray for an open mind so I may come to believe in a Power greater than myself. I pray for humility and the continued opportunity to increase my faith. I don't want to be crazy any more.

94
Third Step Prayer[1]

God, I offer myself to Thee—to build with me and to do with me as Thou wilt. Relieve me of the bondage of self, that I may better do Thy will. Take away my difficulties, that victory over them may bear witness to those I would help of Thy Power, Thy Love, and Thy Way of life. May I do Thy will always!

95
Fourth Step Prayer

Dear God,
It is I who has made my life a mess. I have done it, and I cannot undo it. My mistakes are mine, and I will begin a searching and fearless moral inventory. I will write down my wrongs, but I will also include that which is good. I pray for the strength to complete the task.

1. *Alcoholics Anonymous*, 4th ed., published by AA World Services, Inc., New York, N.Y., p. 63.

96
Fifth Step Prayer

Higher Power, my inventory has shown me who I
am, yet I ask for Your help in admitting my wrongs
to another person and to You. Assure me, and be
with me in this Step, for without this Step I cannot
progress in my recovery. With Your help, I can do
this, and I will do it.

97
Sixth Step Prayer

Dear God,
I am ready for Your help in removing from me the
defects of character which I now realize are obstacles to my recovery. Help me to continue being
honest with myself and guide me toward spiritual
and mental health.

98
Seventh Step Prayer [2]

My Creator, I am now willing that You should have all of me, good and bad. I pray that You now remove from me every single defect of character which stands in the way of my usefulness to You and my fellows. Grant me strength, as I go out from here to do Your bidding. Amen.

99
Eighth Step Prayer

Higher Power, I ask Your help in making my list of all those I have harmed. I will take responsibility for my mistakes, and be forgiving to others just as You are forgiving to me. Grant me the willingness to begin my restitution. This I pray.

2. *Alcoholics Anonymous*, 4th ed., published by AA World Services, Inc., New York, N.Y., p. 76.

100
Ninth Step Prayer

Higher Power, I pray for the right attitude to make my amends, being ever mindful not to harm others in the process. I ask for Your guidance in making indirect amends. Most important, I will continue to make amends by staying abstinent, helping others, and growing in spiritual progress.

101
Tenth Step Prayer

I pray I may continue:
To grow in understanding and effectiveness;
To take daily spot-check inventories of myself;
To correct mistakes when I make them;
To take responsibility for my actions;
To be ever aware of my negative and self-defeating
    attitudes and behaviors;
To keep my willfulness in check;
To always remember I need Your help;
To keep love and tolerance of others as my code;
And to continue in daily prayer how I can best serve
    You, my Higher Power.

102
Eleventh Step Prayer

Higher Power, as I understand You, I pray to keep open my connection with You and to keep it clear from the confusion of daily life. Through my prayers and meditations I ask especially for freedom from self-will, rationalization, and wishful thinking. I pray for the guidance of correct thought and positive action. Your will, Higher Power, not mine, be done.

103
Twelfth Step Prayer

Dear God,

My spiritual awakening continues to unfold. The help I have received I shall pass on and give to others, both in and out of the Fellowship. For this opportunity I am grateful.

I pray most humbly to continue walking day by day on the road of spiritual progress. I pray for the inner strength and wisdom to practice the principles of this way of life in all I do and say. I need You, my friends, and the Program every hour of every day. This is a better way to live.

104
Meeting Prayer No. 1

Our Father, we come to you as a friend.

You have said that, where two or three are gathered in Your name, there You will be in the midst. We believe You are with us now.

We believe this is something You would have us do, and that it has Your blessing.

We believe that You want us to be real partners with you in this business of living, accepting our full responsibility, and certain that the rewards will be freedom, and growth, and happiness.

For this, we are grateful.

We ask You, at all times, to guide us.

Help us daily to come closer to you, and grant us new ways of living our gratitude.

105
Meeting Prayer No. 2

Our Heavenly Father, we ask for Your blessings on this meeting.

Please bless the spirit and the purpose of this group,

Give us strength to follow this Program according
to Your will and in all humility.
Forgive us for yesterday, and grant us courage for
today and hope for tomorrow.

106
Meeting Prayer No. 3

God bless this meeting and the members gathered
here tonight.

Help us to make this group a haven of strength
and comfort, giving to all who seek help here the
beauty and friendliness of home, which shall be as a
shield against temptation of all kinds and against
loneliness and despair.

Bless those who are going forth from this house
to fight the gallant fight, to know suffering; and
bless those who come here to rest, those who must
readjust themselves to face life once more.

107
Amazing Grace

Amazing grace! How sweet the sound
That saved a wretch like me.
I once was lost, but now am found,
Was blind, but now I see.

'Twas grace that taught my heart to fear,
And grace my fears relieved.
How precious did that grace appear
The hour I first believed.

Through many dangers, toils, and snares,
I have already come.
'Tis grace has brought me safe thus far,
And grace will lead me home.

When we've been here ten thousand years,
Bright shining as the sun,
We've no less days to sing God's praise
Than when we'd first begun.

108
High Flight

Oh, I have slipped the surly bonds of earth
And danced the skies on laughter-silvered wings,
Sunward I've climbed and joined the tumbling mirth
Of sun-split clouds—and done a hundred things
You have not dreamed of—wheeled and soared and
    swung
High in the sunlit silence. Hov'ring there
I've chased the shouting wind along and flung
My eager craft through footless halls of air.
Up, up the long, delirious, burning blue
I've topped the windswept heights with easy grace
Where never lark nor even eagle flew.
And, while with silent, lifting mind I've trod
The high untrespassed sanctity of space,
Put out my hand, and touched the face of God.

109
Search for Serenity

The search is yours and mine. Each finds his way
with help, but yet alone.

Serenity is the goal. It comes to those who learn to wait and grow; for each can learn to understand himself and say, "I've found a joy in being me, and knowing you; a knowledge of the depths I can descend, a chance to climb the heights above my head."

The way is not so easy all the time. Our feet will stumble often as we go. A friend may need to give some extra help, as we once gave to others when in the hour of fear.

This is no picnic path that we have found; but yet compared to other days and other times, it seems a better route.

We lost our way before, in fear, guilt, and resentments held too long. Self-pity had its way with us; we found the perfect alibi for all our faults.

We do not know what life may bring from day to day. Tomorrow is a task not yet begun, and we could fail to pass its test.

But this will wait, while in today we do the best we can. Today we try to grow. Today we live, we seek to know, to give, to share, with you.

Yesterday, Today, Tomorrow

There are two days in every week about which we should not worry, two days which should be kept free from fear and apprehension.

One of these days is YESTERDAY with its mistakes and cares, its faults and blunders, its aches and pains. YESTERDAY has passed forever beyond our control.

All the money in the world cannot bring back YESTERDAY. We cannot undo a single act we performed; we cannot erase a single word we said. YESTERDAY is gone.

The other day we should not worry about is TOMORROW with its possible adversaries, its burdens, its large and poor performance. TOMORROW is also beyond our immediate control.

TOMORROW's sun will rise, either in splendor or behind a mask of clouds—but it will rise. Until it does, we have no stake in TOMORROW, for it is as yet unborn.

This leaves only one day . . . TODAY. Any person can fight the battle of just one day. It is only when you and I add the YESTERDAY and TOMORROW that we break down.

It is not the experience of TODAY that drives people mad—it is remorse or bitterness for something which happened YESTERDAY and the dread of what TOMORROW may bring.

LET US, THEREFORE, LIVE BUT ONE DAY AT A TIME!

111
Just for Today

Just for today I will try to live through this day only, and not tackle my whole life problem at once. I can do something for twelve hours that would appall me if I felt that I had to keep it up for a lifetime.

Just for today I will be happy. This assumes to be true what Abraham Lincoln said, that "Most folks are as happy as they make their minds to be."

Just for today I will try to strengthen my mind. I will study; I will learn something useful; I will not be a mental loafer; I will read something that requires effort, thought, and concentration.

Just for today I will exercise my soul in three ways: I will do somebody a good turn, and not get found out; if anybody knows of it, it will not count. I will do at least two things I don't want to do—just for exercise. I will not show anyone that my feelings are hurt; they may be hurt, but today I will not show it.

Just for today I will be agreeable. I will look as good as I can, dress becomingly, talk low, act courteously, criticize not one bit, not find fault with anything, and not try to improve or regulate anybody except myself.

Just for today I will have a program. I may not follow it exactly, but I will have it. I will save myself from two pests: hurry and indecision.

Just for today I will have a quiet half hour all by myself, and relax. During this half hour, sometime, I will try to get a better perspective on my life.

Just for today I will be unafraid. I will enjoy that which is beautiful, and will believe that as I give to the world, so the world will give to me.

112
Footprints

One night a man had a dream. He dreamed he was walking along the beach with the Lord. Across the sky flashed scenes from his life. For each scene, he noticed two sets of footprints in the sand; one belonging to him, and the other to the Lord.

When the last scene of his life flashed before him, he looked back at the footprints in the sand.

He noticed that many times along the path of his life there was only one set of footprints. He also noticed that it happened at the very lowest and saddest times in his life.

This really bothered him and he questioned the Lord about it. "Lord, You said that once I decided to follow You, You'd walk with me all the way. But I have noticed that during the most troublesome times in my life, there is only one set of footprints. I don't understand why when I needed You most You would leave me."

The Lord replied, "My precious, precious child, I love you and I would never leave you. During your times of trial and suffering, when you see only one set of footprints, it was then that I carried you."

113
Desiderata

Go placidly amid the noise and haste, and remember what peace there may be in silence. As far as possible, without surrender, be on good terms with all persons. Speak your truth quietly and clearly; and listen to others, even the dull and ignorant; they, too, have their story.

Avoid loud and aggressive persons; they are vexations to the spirit. If you compare yourself with others, you may become vain and bitter; for always there will be greater and lesser persons than yourself. Enjoy your achievements as well as your plans.

Keep interested in your own career, however humble; it is a real possession in the changing fortunes of time. Exercise caution in your business affairs; for the world is full of trickery. But let this not blind you to what virtue there is; many persons strive for high ideals; and everywhere life is full of heroism.

Be yourself. Especially, do not feign affection. Neither be cynical about love; for in the face of all aridity and disenchantment it is perennial as the grass.

Take kindly the counsel of the years, gracefully surrendering the things of youth. Nurture strength of spirit to shield you in sudden misfortune. But do not distress yourself with imaginings. Many fears are born of fatigue and loneliness. Beyond a wholesome discipline, be gentle with yourself.

You are a child of the universe, no less than the trees and the stars; you have a right to be here. And whether or not it is clear to you, no doubt the universe is unfolding as it should.

Therefore be at peace with God, whatever you conceive Him to be, and whatever your labors and aspirations, in the noisy confusion of life, keep peace with your soul.

With all its sham, drudgery, and broken dreams, it is still a beautiful world. Strive to be happy.

114
Letting Go

As children bring their broken toys
With tears for us to mend,
I brought my broken dreams to God,
Because God is my friend.
But then, instead of leaving my Higher Power
In peace to work alone,
I hung around and tried to help,
With ways that were my own.
At last, I snatched them back and cried,
"How can You be so slow?"
"My child," God said, "what could I do?
You never did let go."

The Letter

Dear Friend,

How are you? I just had to send a note to tell you how much I care about you.

I saw you yesterday as you were talking with your friends. I waited all day hoping you would want to talk to me too. I gave you a sunset to close your day and a cool breeze to rest you—and I waited. You never came. It hurt me, but I still love you because I am your friend.

I saw you sleeping last night and longed to touch your brow, so I spilled moonlight upon your face. Again I waited, wanting to rush down so we could talk. I have so many gifts for you! You awoke and rushed off to work. My tears were in the rain.

If you would only listen to me! I love you! I try to tell you in blue skies and in the quiet green grass. I whisper it in leaves on the trees and breathe it in colors of flowers, shout it to you in mountain streams, give the birds love songs to sing. My love for you is deeper than the ocean, and bigger than the biggest need in your heart!

Ask me! Talk to me! Please don't forget me! I have so much to share with you!

I won't hassle you any further. It is *your* decision.
I have chosen you and I will wait.

I love you. Your friend,
God

116
Live a Little, Just to Please

Can you say today in honesty
As the hours slip by so fast,
That you've helped a single person
Of the many you have passed?

Did you waste the day, or lose it?
Was it well or properly spent?
Did you leave a trail of kindness
Or mementos of discontent?

Have you given God a moment
In humble, devout prayer?
Have you talked with Him in honesty
To let Him know you care?

As you close your eyes in slumber,
Do you think that God would say,
"You have made the world much better,
For you **lived a lot** today?"

117
I Am Me

In all of the world, there is no one else exactly like
me. Everything that comes out of me is authentically
mine because I alone choose it. I own everything
about me: my body, my feelings, my mouth, my
voice, all my actions, whether they be to others or
to myself. I own my fantasies, my dreams, my hopes,
my fears. I own all of my triumphs and successes, all
of my failures and mistakes.

Because I own all of me, I can become intimately
acquainted with me. By doing so, I can love me and
be friendly with me in all of my parts. I know there
are aspects about myself that puzzle me, and other
aspects that I do not know, but as long as I am
friendly and loving to myself, I can courageously
look for solutions to the puzzles and for ways to find
out more about me.

However I look and sound, whatever I say and

do, and whatever I think and feel at a given moment in time is authentically me. If later some parts of how I looked, sounded, thought, and felt turn out to be unfitting, I can discard that which is unfitting, keep the rest, and invent something new for that which I discarded. I can see, hear, feel, think, say, and do. I have the tools to survive, to be close to others, to be productive, and to make sense and order out of the world of people and things outside of me, and therefore I can engineer me. I am me and I am okay.

118
Don't Quit

When things go wrong as they sometimes will,
When the road you're trudging seems all uphill,
When the funds are low and the debts are high,
And you want to smile, but you have to sigh;
When care is pressing you down a bit,
Rest, if you must, but don't quit.
Life is funny with its twists and turns,
As every one of us sometimes learns;
And many a failure has turned about
When they might have won had they stuck it out.

Don't give up though the pace seems slow;
You may succeed with another blow.
Success is failure turned inside out;
The silver tint of the clouds of doubt.
And you can never tell how close you are;
It may be near when it seems so far.
So stick to the fight when you're hardest hit.
It's when things seem worst that you must not quit.

119
My Medallion

I always carry my medallion,
A simple reminder to me
Of the fact that I'm in recovery
No matter where I may be.

This little chip is not magic
Nor is it a good luck charm.
It isn't supposed to protect me
From every possible harm.

It's not meant for comparison,
Or for all the world to see,
It's simply an understanding
Between my Higher Power and me.

Whenever I doubt the cost
I paid for recovery,
I look at my medallion
To remember what used to be.

It reminds me to be thankful
For my blessings day by day,
And to practice the principles
In all I do and say.

It's also a daily reminder
Of the peace and comfort I share
With all who work the Program
And show they really care.

So I carry my medallion
To remind no one but me
That the Promises will unfold
If I let God work for me.

I Didn't Have Time

I got up early one morning
And rushed right into the day.
I had so much to accomplish
That I didn't have time to pray.
Problems just tumbled about me
And heavier came each task.
"Why doesn't God help me," I wondered.
He answered, "You didn't ask."
I wanted to see joy and beauty
But the day toiled on, gray and bleak.
I wondered why God didn't show me.
He said, "But you didn't seek."
I tried to come into God's presence;
I used all my keys at the lock.
God gently and lovingly chided,
"My child, you didn't knock."
I woke up early this morning
And paused before entering the day.
I had so much to accomplish
That I had to take time to pray.

121
Someone Does Care

I found God in the morning; we just sat and talked.
I kept Him near me, everywhere I walked.
I called on God at noontime, a heart filled with
   despair.
I felt His quiet presence; I knew He was there.
We met again at sunset, the waning of the day.
I had made Him happy; I had lived His way.
Then when at bedtime I knelt silently in prayer,
Again His gentle presence I felt. Someone does care.

122
Resent Somebody

The moment you start to resent a person you become that person's slave. He or she controls your dreams, absorbs your digestion, robs you of your peace of mind and good will, and takes away the pleasure of your work.

A person you resent ruins your spirituality and nullifies your prayers. You cannot take a vacation without that person going along! He or she destroys your freedom of mind and hounds you wherever you go. There is no way to escape the person you resent.

That person is with you when you are awake and invades your privacy when you sleep. That person is close beside you when you eat, when you drive your car, and when you are on the job.

You can never have efficiency or happiness. The person you resent influences even the tone of your voice. He or she requires you to take medicine for indigestion, headaches, and loss of energy. That person even steals your last moment of consciousness before you go to sleep.

So if you want to be a slave, harbor your resentments.

123
Living the Way We Pray

I knelt to pray when day was done
And prayed: "O Lord, bless everyone,
And lift from each heart the pain,
And let the sick be well again."

And then the next day when I did awake,
I carelessly went on my way.

The whole day long I did not try
To wipe a tear from any eye.

I did not try to share the load
Of any brother on the road.
I did not even go to see
The sick man just next door to me.

Yet once again when day was done
I prayed: "O Lord, bless everyone."
But as I prayed, to my ear
There came a voice that whispered clear:

"Pause, hypocrite, before you pray:
Whom have you tried to bless today?
God's sweetest blessings always go
By hands that serve Him here below."

124
Love Is

Love is friendship that has caught fire. It is quiet
understanding, mutual confidence, sharing, and forgiving. It is loyalty through good times and bad. It

settles for less than perfection and makes allowances for human weaknesses.

Love is content with the present, it hopes for the future, and it doesn't brood over the past. It's the day-in-and-day-out chronicle of irritations, problems, compromises, small disappointments, big victories, and common goals.

If you have love in your life, it can make up for a great many things you lack. If you don't have it, no matter what else there is it's not enough.

125
Happiness

Happiness is not a matter of good fortune or worldly possessions. It's a mental attitude. It comes from appreciating what we have, instead of being miserable about what we don't have. It's so simple— yet so difficult for the human mind to comprehend.

126
My Bill of Rights

I have the right to be treated with respect.
I have the right to say no and not feel guilty.
I have the right to experience and express my feelings.
I have the right to take time for myself.
I have the right to change my mind.
I have the right to ask for what I want.
I have the right to ask for information.
I have the right to make mistakes.
I have the right to do less than I am humanly
    capable of.
I have the right to feel good about myself.
I have the right to act only in ways that promote my
    dignity and self-respect as long as others are not
    violated in the process.

127
Walk with Me

Don't walk in front of me . . . I may not follow.
Don't walk behind me . . . I may not lead.
Just walk beside me and be my friend.

128
It Shows in Your Face

You don't have to tell how you live each day;
You don't have to say if you work or play;
A tired, true barometer serves in the place.
However you live, it shows in your face.

The falseness, the deceit that you wear in your heart
Will not stay inside where it got its start;
For sinew and blood is a thin veil of lace.
However you live, it shows in your face.

If you have battled and won in the game of life,
If you feel you've conquered the sorrow and strife,
If you've played the game square and you stand on
   first base,
You don't have to tell it, it shows in your face.

If your life's been unselfish, for others you live,
And not what you get, but what you can give,
And you live close to God, in His infinite Grace,
You don't have to tell it, it shows in your face.

The Touch of the Master's Hand

It was battered and scarred and the auctioneer
Thought it scarcely worth his while
To waste his time on the old violin,
But he held it up with a smile.
"What am I bid, good people?" he cried.
"Who starts the bidding for me?
One dollar? One dollar. Do I hear two?
Two dollars. Who makes it three?
Three dollars once, three dollars twice,
Going for three . . ." But no!
From the room, far back, a gray-bearded man
Came forward and picked up the bow.
Then wiping the dust from the old violin,
And tightening up the strings,
He played a melody, pure and sweet,
As sweet as the angel sings.
The music ceased, and the auctioneer,
With a voice that was quiet and low,
Said, "What now am I bid for this old violin?"
As he held it aloft with its bow.
"One thousand? One thousand, do I hear two?
Two thousand. Who makes it three?
Three thousand once, three thousand twice,

Going and gone!" said he.
The audience cheered, but some of them cried,
"We just don't understand.
What changed its worth?" Swift came the reply,
"The touch of the master's hand."
And many a man, with life out of tune,
All battered with bourbon and gin,
Is auctioned cheap, to a thoughtless crowd,
Much like the old violin.
A mess of pottage, a glass of wine,
A game, and he travels on.
He is going once, he is going twice,
He is going, and almost gone.
But the Master comes and the foolish crowd
Never can quite understand
The worth of a soul, the change that is wrought,
By the Touch of the Master's Hand.

130
When Seeking God

If a person would find God, let that person humbly
ask for a chance to believe; and meanwhile let him or
her go personally, not by delegate, to a less fortunate
brother, helping him in his need of body and soul.

When a person seeks God, he or she will presently find what is sought. For when a person can leave him- or herself and enter the lives of others, that person leaves his or her own heart open so that God may enter and dwell within.

131
One Day at a Time

One day at a time—this is enough.
Do not look back and grieve over the past, for it is
   gone.
And do not be troubled about the future, for it has
   not yet come.
Live in the present, and make it so beautiful that it
   will be worth remembering.

132
Risk

To laugh is to risk appearing the fool.
To weep is to risk being called sentimental.

To reach out to another is to risk involvement.
To expose feelings is to risk showing your true self.
To place your ideas and dreams before the crowd is
    to risk being called naïve.
To love is to risk not being loved in return.
To live is to risk dying.
To hope is to risk despair.
To try is to risk failure.
But risks must be taken,
Because the greatest risk in life is to risk nothing.
The people who risk nothing do nothing,
Have nothing, are nothing, and become nothing.
They may avoid suffering and sorrow,
But they simply cannot learn to feel,
And change, and grow, and love, and live.
Chained by their servitude, they are slaves;
They have forfeited their freedom.
Only the people who risk are truly free.

133
Thy Will Be Done

If I were to chase each particular care, each particular worry, and each particular sorrow, I would have business on hand for the rest of my life; but if I can rise into a higher state of mind, these cease to be annoyances and cares. Ninety-nine parts in a hundred of the cares of life are cured by one single salve, and that is, "Thy will be done." The moment I can say that, and let go, that moment more than ninety-nine parts in a hundred of my troubles drop away.

134
Comes the Dawn

After a while you learn the subtle difference between holding a hand and chaining a soul. And you learn that love doesn't mean leaning and company doesn't mean security. And you begin to learn that kisses aren't contracts, and presents aren't promises.

And you begin to accept your defeats with your head up and your eyes open, with the grace of a grown-up, not the grief of a child.

And you learn to build all your roads on today because tomorrow's ground is too uncertain for plans, and futures have a way of falling down in mid-flight.

After a while you learn that even sunshine burns if you get too much. So you plant your own garden and decorate your own soul, instead of waiting for someone to bring you flowers.

And you learn that you really can endure, that you really are strong, and you really do have worth.

And you learn and learn. . . . With every good-bye, you learn.

————————————

135
God's Presence

I met God in the morning
When my day was at its best,
And His presence came like sunrise,
Like a glory in my breast.

All day long this presence lingered,
All day long He stayed with me,
And we sailed in perfect calmness
O'er a very troubled sea.

Other ships were torn and battered;
Other ships were sore distressed;
But the winds that seemed to drive them
Brought me to a peace and rest.

Then I thought of other mornings
With a keen remorse of mind,

When I, too, had loosed the moorings
With this presence left behind.

So I think I've found the secret
Learned through many a troubled way:
You must meet God in the morning
If you want Him through the day.

136
Time Somebody Told Me

Time somebody told me
That I am lovely, good, and real.
That my beauty could make hearts stand still.

Time somebody told me
That my love is total and so complete,
That my mind is quick and full of wit,
That my loving is just too good to quit.

Time somebody told me
How much a person wants, loves, and needs me,
How much my spirit helps set that person free,
How my eyes shine full of the white light,

How good it feels just to hold me tight.
Time somebody told me.

So I had a talk with myself,
Just me, nobody else,
'Cause it *was* time somebody told me.

137
Rejecting Rejection

"God don't make junk." In other words, every person
has an infinite spiritual worth that has nothing to do
with the ordinary judgments of the marketplace and
the world. Other people may reject us for both
good and bad reasons, but the real Source of our
existence will never turn us away.

Moreover, this Higher Power is also capable of
leading each of us to the people and places that fit
our needs and our social talents for service. Many of
us who are now in recovery feel that this happened
when we were being led to the Fellowship.

138
The Peace of Meditation

So we may know God better
And feel His quiet power,
Let us daily keep in silence
A meditation hour.
For to understand God's greatness
And to use His gifts each day,
The soul must learn to meet Him
In a meditative way.
For our Father tells His children
That if they would know His will.
They must seek Him in the silence
When all is calm and still.

For nature's greatest forces
Are found in quiet things,
Like softly falling snowflakes
Drifting down on angels' wings,
Or petals dropping soundlessly
From a lovely full-blown rose.
God comes closest to us
When our souls are in repose.
So let us plan with prayerful care
To always allocate
A certain portion of each day
To be still and meditate.

The Bike Ride

At first I saw God as my observer, my judge, keeping track of the things I did wrong, so as to know whether I merited heaven or hell when I die. He was out there sort of like the President. I recognized His picture when I saw it, but I didn't really know Him.

But later on when I recognized my Higher Power, it seemed as though life was rather like a bike ride; but it was a tandem bike, and I noticed that God was in the back helping me pedal.

I don't know just when it was that He suggested we change places, but life has not been the same since . . . life with my Higher Power, that is. God makes life exciting.

When I had control, I knew the way. It was rather boring, but predictable. It was the shortest distance between two points.

But when He took the lead, He knew delightful long cuts, up mountains, and through rocky places and at breakneck speeds. It was all I could do to hang on! Even though it looked like madness, He said "pedal."

I worried and was anxious and asked, "Where are You taking me?" He laughed and didn't answer, and I started to trust.

I forgot my boring life and entered into the

adventure; and when I'd say, "I'm scared," He'd lean back and touch my hand.

He took me to people with gifts that I needed, gifts of healing, acceptance, and joy. They gave me their gifts to take on my journey; our journey, God's and mine.

And we were off again. He said, "Give the gifts away. They're extra baggage, too much weight." So I did, to the people we met, and I found that in giving I received, and still our burden was light.

I did not trust Him at first, in control of my life. I thought He'd wreck it. But He knew bike secrets, knew how to make it bend to take sharp corners, jump to clear high places filled with rocks, fly to shorten scary passages.

And I'm learning to shut up and pedal in the strangest places, and I'm beginning to enjoy the view and the cool breeze on my face with my delightful constant companion, my Higher Power.

And when I'm sure I can't do any more, He just smiles and says, "PEDAL!"

140
This Day

This is the day which the Lord has made; let us rejoice and be glad in it.

Psalm 118:24

141
The Great Reality

Let the Great Reality govern my every thought, and Truth be the heart of my life. For so it must be for all of humanity. Please help me to do "my part." And may the intensity of all our egos become the Joy of our One Soul.

142
The Morning Light

Lord of the night,
Be with me through the hours of darkness.
Let all my questions,
Problems, decisions,
Be enveloped in sleep
That through the mystery
Of the sleeping mind
The difficulties of this day
Will be seen to be easier
In the morning light.
Into Your hands, O Lord,
I commit my spirit.

143
Rest

Go with each of us to rest;
If we awake, temper to them the dark hours of
    watching;
And when the day returns, return to us,
Our Sun and Comforter, and call us up with
Morning faces and with morning hearts

Eager to labor, eager to be happy
If happiness would be our portion,
And if the day be marked for sorrow,
We are strong to endure it.

144
One More Day

We carry the solution within us.
All that comes our way is blessed.
The Great Spirit gives us one more day.
We silence our fearful mind.

Do not wait to open our hearts.
Let us flow with the Mystery.
Sometimes the threads have no weave.
The price of not loving ourselves is high.

145
Our True Home

Our true home is in the present moment.
To live in the present moment is a miracle.

The miracle is not to walk on water.
The miracle is to walk on the green earth in the
   present moment,
To appreciate the peace and beauty that are avail-
   able now.
Peace is all around us—
In the world and in nature—
And within us—
In our bodies and our spirits.
Once we learn to touch this peace,
We will be healed and transformed.
It is not a matter of faith;
It is a matter of practice.

_____

146
Blessing for Partners
(Apache Blessing)

Now you will feel no rain,
For each of you will be shelter for the other.

Now you will feel no cold,
For each of you will be warmth to the other.

Now there will be no loneliness,
For each of you will be companion to the other.

Now you are two persons,
But there is only one life before you.

May beauty surround you both
In journey ahead and through all the years.

May happiness be your companion and
Your days together will be good and long upon
    the earth.

147
Who Are You to Say There Is No God?[3]

As I reflected on this question I tumbled out of bed
    to my knees.
I am overwhelmed by a conviction of the presence
    of God.

3. Adapted from *Alcoholics Anonymous*, 4th ed., published by
AA World Services, Inc., New York, N.Y., p. 56.

It pours through me with the certainty and majesty
　　of a great tide at flood.
The barriers I have built denying Your Spirit
　　through the years are swept away.
I stand now in the presence of Your Infinite Power
　　and Love.
I have stepped from bridge to shore.
For the first time, I live in conscious companionship
　　with my Creator.

148
Our Possessions

Father of Light, teach us to value our possessions in
　　the right way.
Help us never to think more of them than of people.
Make us ready to use them freely for the good of
　　others
And to share them generously without complaining.
Thank You for the beautiful things we enjoy
　　possessing.
May our enjoyment be wholesome and right and
　　may we hold to all we own.

149
Serene Days

God of the seas, to You I pray:
Bless unto me these serene days.

From these wide seas give unto me
A larger heart of charity.

May these strong tides wash out my mind
From all that's bitter and unkind.

With the broad beat of seabird's wings
Lift up my soul to heavenly things.

By the far sight of hills untrod
Call me to undared ventures, God.

Grant that these serene days may be
Your holy days indeed to me.

150
Dwell in My Heart

O God, dwell in my heart,
Open it out, purify it, make it bright and beautiful,

Awaken it, prepare it, make it fearless,
Make it a blessing to others,
Rid it of laziness, free it from doubt,
Unite it with all, destroy its bondage,
Let Your peaceful music pervade all its works.
Make my heart useful to You and others.

151
For Families Torn by Addiction

We pray, O God of hope,
For all families
Whose lives are torn and disrupted
By addiction.
Enable them to identify the illness.
Strengthen them to seek help.
Bless them with the power of Your love,
Which imparts transformation and wholeness
To those who trust in Your name.
Grant that as they walk this tortured road,
They may journey together
And bind close in the bond of love.
Amen.

152
Wesley P.'s Prayer

Dear God, please fill me
With Your loving spirit, and
Let it flow through me
Into the lives of others.
Amen.

153
Set Aside Prayer

Lord, today help me set aside
    everything I think I know about You
Everything I think I know
    about myself
Everything I think I know
    about others and
Everything I think I know
    about my own recovery
For a new experience in myself
A new experience in my fellows
    and my own recovery.

154
Usefulness Prayer

God, help me today to find balance
Between my character defects and the
Principles of our Program
So as, to be useful
To myself, all others, and You,
The God of my understanding.

155
Prayer during Turmoil

Dear Higher Power,
During times when my world becomes unhinged
And the foundations of what I believe crack and
    dissolve,
Give me the grace to believe that Your power is at
    work in the turmoil of my life.
Lead me to remember that Your power is greater
    than all evil,
And though the world may rock and sometimes
    break,
It will in time be transformed by Your Love.

156
Next Right Step

God, please show me all through this day,
What is the next right step.
Give me the strength, faith, and courage
I need to take care of the problems in my life.
Show me the solutions, for I will take the
Next right actions. And, I ask to be free
From self-will and fear. Your will, not mine,
Be done. Amen.

157
Mychal's Prayer[4]

Lord, take me where You want me to go;
Let me meet who You want me to meet;
Tell me what You want me to say;
And
Keep me out of Your way.

4. Father Mychal Judge, NYC Fire Department Chaplain,
   killed September 11, 2001.

158
Free of Resentment Prayer

God, free me from my resentment
Toward _____.
Please bless _____ in whatever it is that You know
They may be needing this day.
Please give _____ everything I want for myself.
And may _____'s life be full of health, peace,
Prosperity, and happiness as they seek to have
A closer relationship with You.

159
The Fear Prayer

God, thank You for helping me to be honest
Enough to see the truth about myself.
Thank You for showing me my fears,
Please help me remove them.
Help me outgrow my fears;
The fears that have haunted me
And blocked me from doing Your will.
Direct my attention to what You
Would have me be.

Demonstrate through me and
Help me do Your will always.

160
Cleveland AA Prayer, 1941

God, You have been our dwelling place in all
    generations.
Before the mountains were brought forth, or even
    the earth and the world were made.
We thank You for having brought us safely to this
    day of our lives and
Having taught us to live one day at a time in Your
    work.
We pray that You will guide our footsteps tomorrow,
    and help us as we help ourselves, help us as we
    help others to do Your will.
And we pray that You will extend your special
    mercy to those afflicted, as we have been, but
    who have not yet been brought from darkness
    to light.

161
In Fellowship

Whatever is true, whatever is noble,

Whatever is right, whatever is pure, whatever is
lovely,

Whatever is unselfish—if anything is useful or
praiseworthy—

I will think about such things.

The things I have learned and received and heard
and seen in

Our Fellowship and Program, I will practice, and the
God of

My understanding will be with me.

162
Surrender Prayer
(Oxford Group, 1934)

I surrender to You my entire life, O God.

I have made a mess of it, trying to run it myself.

You take it—the whole thing—and run it for me,

According to Your will and plan.

163
Right Living

From the cowardice that dare not face new truth
From the laziness that is contented with half-truth
From the arrogance that thinks it knows all truth,
Good Lord, deliver me.

164
Peace in Our Hearts

Our Creator, show us the way of patience,
    tolerance,
And kindness. Grant us power in our love,
Strength in our humility,
Clarity in our thinking,
Purity in our zeal,
Sincerity in our purpose,
Kindness in our laughter,
Value in our gratitude,
Compassion in our friendships,
And Your peace in our hearts at all times.

165
Our Meeting Room Door

Dear God,
Make the door of this meeting wide enough
To receive all who need love and fellowship
And narrow enough to shut out
All envy, pride, and hate.
Make its threshold smooth enough
To be no stumbling block to anyone,
Nor to those who have strayed,
But rugged enough to turn back
The tempter's power:
Make it a gateway
To Thine eternal kingdom.

166
Honest and Sincere

Dear God,

Help me to realize this day that it is Your will,
Not mine that is to be done, and then to do it.

Help me to accept myself as I am,
But to constantly hope that I may become better.

Help me to forgive, to love, and to accept others
But to ask for absolutely nothing in return.

Help me to be grateful for what I have and to accept
More only if You will it.

Help me to receive tenderness as well as to give it.

Help me to be honest and sincere with myself,
But to remember with a smile how little I am.

Help me, above all, to have utter faith in You as
My friend and leader.

Help me to re-create the mood of this prayer
Every twenty-four hours.

167
Wedding Blessing

All knowing spirit, Higher Power, join us in this
ceremony binding the lives of these two people. We

ask a blessing on this couple, on their marriage, and on the life they will lead together. As they speak and we hear the words that will forever join them, allow the intentions being uttered to remain true through time and to run as deep as a singing river throughout the landscape of their lives.

168
No Fear

I am a child of God
In God I live and move and have my being
So I have no fear
I am surrounded by the peace of God
And all is well
I am not afraid of people—
I am not afraid of things—
I am not afraid of circumstances—
I am not afraid of sickness
For God is with me
The peace of God fills my soul
And I have no fear.

169
Kindness Prayer

Keep us, O God, from closed mindedness; let us
Be large in thought, in word, in deed.
Let us be done with faultfinding, and
Leave off self-seeking.
May we put away all pretense and
Meet each other face-to-face, without
Self-pity and without prejudice.
May we never be hasty in our judgment
And be always generous and helpful.
Teach us to put into action our better
Impulses, straightforward and unafraid.
Let us take time for the right things. Make us
Grow calm, serene, and gentle.
Grant that we may realize it is the
Little things that create difference,
That in the big things in life we are one.
And may we strive to touch and know
The great common heart of us all;
And O God, let us not forget to be kind.

Eleventh Step Meeting
Opening Prayer

God,

We come together to fulfill a call to community and
to nurture one another into Being.

To practice engaging in God within ourselves and
one another.

To share the way we live, love, struggle, and dare to
be, that this community will be inspiring to ourselves and others.

We pray to vigilantly seek within ourselves a God
Presence that enables us to embrace our humanity and to step into the Spiritual Experience of
mindfully living fully, loving wastefully, and entering courageously into the depths of Being.

We pray to be more adequately God-bearers—a
source of life, love, and Being to others.

To be changed, opened, sensitized, and
compassionate.

To witness to one another the profound ways that
prayer and meditation have changed us.

To share the healing Power of God which is Love.

Our prayer is a conscious recognition that God is
Love, and God is a Power that calls us more

deeply into the mystery of Being and into a fuller
humanity.

We pray to know that we are in God, that God is in
us, that God heals, and that God alone fulfills our
shared longing.

We especially pray to know that God is our only
source.

We give thanks for our personal relationship
with God.

Amen.

171
Paul D.'s Prayer

We thank You, dear Lord, for giving us Bill and Dr.
Bob and for Your divine guidance and direction in
their creation of our Fellowship and Program.

We thank You, dear Lord, for Your blessings and
protection of our Fellowship and our Program over
the past sixty years and we pray, dear Lord, that You
will continue to bless and protect our Fellowship
and our Program of Alcoholics Anonymous, always.
We thank You, dear Lord, for the countless number
of alcoholics for whom You have lifted the bonds of

alcohol and allowed us to get sober, live sober lives, and die sober deaths.

We pray, dear Lord, that You will hear the prayers and the cry for help from the still sick and suffering alcoholics and send them to us.

We pray, dear Lord, that we remain forever humble and grateful and always worthy to receive and keep this precious gift of sobriety that You have bestowed upon us, and for all the benefits, gifts, and many, many blessings that we have received from the Program of Alcoholics Anonymous, we thank You, dear Lord.

172
No Standing Still

Spirit of the Universe, never let me think that I have knowledge enough to need no teaching, wisdom enough to need no correction, talents enough to need no grace, goodness enough to need no progress, humility enough to need no repentance, devotion enough to need no inspiration, strength sufficient without Your Spirit; fearing, if I stand still, I will fall back for evermore.

173
The Gift of Humility

Grant upon us, O God, the gift of humility. When
we speak, teach us to give our opinion quietly and
sincerely. When we do well in work or play, give
us a sense of proportion, that we be neither unduly
elated nor foolishly self-deprecatory. Help us in success to realize what we owe to You and the efforts of
others; in failure, to avoid self-pity; and in all ways
to be simple and natural, quiet in manner, and rea-
sonable in thought.

174
My Design

God, my purpose is to help others.
Give me this work,
Till my life shall end
And life
Till my work is done.

175
Darkness to Light

Lord, I believe that You will reward each person according to his or her good works. Thank You for
turning my darkness into light and for comforting
me during my trials and low spots so that I may
comfort and encourage others. Set Your word always
before me so that I might remember Your great and
awesome deeds. You are a faithful and just Teacher.

176
Consciousness of God

I came, at my first surrender, not only into consciousness of God but into usefulness *for* God and
others. I was able to do, through God's help, what
no one has ever been able or ever will be able to
do alone, which is to supplement the all-important
"why" of life with the still more important "how" of
living. I was able to begin solving my own problems
and, for the first time in my experience, was given
the power to begin helping others. I no longer
wished well to "myself alone." Dear God, I pray
to surrender again today.

177
Empty Out

O God, thank You for my spiritual growth and especially that gradual walk into Your light, which has seemed to be a process of breaking down—of disorganization, of emptying out—a matter of deflation in my own self-importance until self-approval and concern for the approval of others has shrunk to a point where I'm willing to step entirely aside and give You a chance to shine.

178
Dick B.'s Prayer

Heavenly Father, I thank and praise You in the name of Jesus Christ, for delivering me from the power of darkness and translating me into the kingdom of Your dear son; for affirming that You are Yahweh, our Creator, who heals all our diseases, forgives all our iniquities, redeems our lives from destruction, and showers us with loving kindness and tender mercies; and who wishes above all things that we prosper and be in health.

I ask Your forgiveness for my sins of today. I ask for the cure of all my infirmities and those of my family and friends. I thank You that by confessing Jesus as my Lord and believing in my heart that You raised Him from the dead, I have become Your son, received remission of past sins, and been healed by Jesus' stripes. I can and do ask that You provide me with the wisdom to choose each day the way of Your will; that You strengthen and guide me to obeying Your will and resisting temptations; and that You lead me to those who hunger for, and want Your salvation and a full and accurate knowledge of Your truth.

I thank You for supplying all my needs; for keeping me, my family, my fellow believers, and friends safe and in perfect soundness, and for protecting and keeping safe our President, his administration, our governments, our service men and women, and our country.

I ask that doing all to Your glory and loving You and my brothers with all my heart, soul, mind, and strength be my hearty and daily service to You. I ask for all these things in the name of Your precious son, Jesus Christ.

179
Heart of a Child

Grant me, O God,
The heart of a child,
Pure and transparent as a spring;
A simple heart,
Which never harbors sorrows;
A heart glorious in self-giving,
Tender in compassion;
A heart faithful and generous,
Which will never forget any good
Or bear a grudge for any evil.

Make me a heart gentle and humble,
Loving without asking in return,
Large-hearted and undauntable,
Which no ingratitude can sour,
And no indifference weary;
A heart born to help others,
Usefulness never measured.

180
Karen C.'s Prayer

Today, I pray, I will:
Talk to someone who can help me;
Own my true destiny;
Compliment someone;
Get to know myself better;
Work to create a promising future;
Take advantage of my opportunities;
Allow myself to feel whole;
Use my support system;
Be honorable in my intentions;
Be inspired by the achievements of others;
Have the courage to own the truth;
Act as if there are no obstacles;
Treat myself and others with respect.
Today and from now on I will end
Every prayer with "Thy will be done."

181
Free from Fear

O God, for another day, for another morning, for
  another hour, for another chance to live and

serve You, I am truly grateful. According to Your
will, this day free me:
From fear of the future;
From anxiety of the morrow;
From bitterness toward anyone;
From cowardice in face of danger;
From laziness in face of work;
From failure before opportunity;
From weakness when Your power is at hand
And fill me with:
Love that knows no barrier;
Courage that cannot be shaken;
Faith through the darkness;
Strength sufficient for my tasks;
Loyalty to the Fellowship;
Wisdom to meet life's complexities.
Be with me another day and use me as You will.

―――――――――――――

182
Searcy W.'s Prayer

I pray today to:
Trust God,
Clean house,
Help others.

183
Blessed Mother Teresa's Prayer

Let nothing upset you;
Let nothing frighten you.
Everything is changing;
God alone is changeless.
Patience attains the goal.
Who has God lacks nothing:
God alone fills all of our needs.

Hazelden Foundation, a national nonprofit organization founded in 1949, helps people reclaim their lives from the disease of addiction. Built on decades of knowledge and experience, Hazelden's comprehensive approach to addiction addresses the full range of individual, family, and professional needs, including addiction treatment and continuing care services for youth and adults, publishing, research, higher learning, public education, and advocacy.

A life of recovery is lived "one day at a time." Hazelden publications, both educational and inspirational, support and strengthen lifelong recovery. In 1954, Hazelden published *Twenty-Four Hours a Day,* the first daily meditation book for recovering alcoholics, and Hazelden continues to publish works to inspire and guide individuals in treatment and recovery, and their loved ones. Professionals who work to prevent and treat addiction also turn to Hazelden for evidence-based curricula, informational materials, and videos for use in schools, treatment programs, and correctional programs.

Through published works, Hazelden extends the reach of hope, encouragement, help, and support to individuals, families, and communities affected by addiction and related issues.

For questions about Hazelden publications, please call **800-328-9000** or visit us online at **hazelden.org/bookstore.**